First World War
and Army of Occupation
War Diary
France, Belgium and Germany

58 DIVISION
Divisional Troops
Royal Army Medical Corps
2/2 Home Counties Field Ambulance
1 September 1915 - 22 February 1916

WO95/2997/3

The Naval & Military Press Ltd
www.nmarchive.com
Published in association with The National Archives

Published by

The Naval & Military Press Ltd

Unit 10 Ridgewood Industrial Park,

Uckfield, East Sussex,

TN22 5QE England

Tel: +44 (0) 1825 749494

www.naval-military-press.com

www.nmarchive.com

This diary has been reprinted in facsimile from the original. Any imperfections are inevitably reproduced and the quality may fall short of modern type and cartographic standards.

© Crown Copyright
Images reproduced by permission of The National Archives, London, England, 2015.

Contents

Document type	Place/Title	Date From	Date To
Heading	WO95/2997-3		
Heading	U K 67 Division To 58 Division 2/2 Home Counties Fld Amb 1915 Aug-1916 Feb		
Miscellaneous	Statement Accompanying War Diary of 2/2nd Home Counties Field Ambulance. R.A.M.C. (T)., For August,1915		
War Diary	Balmer Camp Falmer Sussex	01/09/1915	31/10/1915
War Diary	Kirkella Sevenoaks Kent.	00/11/1915	00/11/1915
War Diary	Sevenoaks	03/11/1915	27/11/1915
War Diary	Kirkella Sevenoaks	07/12/1915	22/02/1916

WO 95/2997/3

UK

67 DIVISION
TO 58 DIVISION

2/2 HOME COUNTIES FLD AMB

1915 AUG — 1916 FEB JAN

STATEMENT ACCOMPANYING WAR DIARY of 2/2nd HOME COUNTIES FIELD AMBULANCE, R.A.M.C.(T)., for AUGUST, 1915. . . . .

Since the last statement I took over Command as from 21/8/15. The routine work of organizing and administering the Field Ambulance has been proceeded with in accordance with Regulations and the training has been carried out according to "R.A.M.C. Training." The sick from the Kent Infantry Brigade have been attended and treated.

Captain.
Officer Commanding
2/2nd H.C.F.AMB. R.A.M.C(T).

Balmer Camp,
   Falmer, Sussex.
      2nd September, 1915.

WAR DIARY or INTELLIGENCE SUMMARY.

(Erase heading not required.)

Army Form C. 2118.

Hour, Date, Place	Summary of Events and Information	Remarks and references to Appendices
1915.		
9-12 a.m. Sept. 1st Balmer	Routine Training; Stretcher Drill for Bearer Section and Lecture for Tent Sub-Section. Orders to complete Med.Hist.Sheets for Men.	
2-4.30 p.m. Camp,	Routine Training; Squad and Stretcher Drill, Lecture, Route March.	
9-12 a.m. 2nd Falmer, SUSSEX.	Transport Inspection.	
2-4.30 p.m. "	Routine Training; Demonstration-of-First-Field-Dressing. Orders to issue Identity Discs to the Men. Brigade Route March.	
9-12 a.m. 3rd "		
2-4.30 p.m. "	Routine Training; Demonstration of First Field Dressing; Kit Inspection. Roll Call showing state of Vaccination called for.	
9-12 a.m. 4th "		
9.30 a.m. 5th "	Church parade.	
9-12 a.m. 6th "	Routine Training; Striking and Pitching Tents; Route March.	
2-4.30 p.m. "	Routine Training; Stretcher and First Aid Work. Medical History Sheets for Men completed.	
9-12 a.m. 7th "		
2-4.30 p.m. "	Routine Training; Roller Bandaging, Stretcher and Wagon Drill. Route March.	
9-12 a.m. 8th "		
2-4.30 p.m. "	Routine Training; Company Drill, R.A.M.C. Training, Route March. Transport Inspection. Nursing duties taken over by "B" Section.	
9-12 a.m. 9th "	Routine Training in the morning. Capt.Alston appointed Senior Medical Officer to 201st Midd.Inf.Bde. after departure of Lieut.Col.Warrack, 1/1st H.C.C.C.S., on 9th inst. (Auth: A.D.M.S. 3290,8/9/15).	
2-4.30 p.m. 10th "	Routine Training; R.A.M.C. Training, Physical Drill, Kit Inspection. Order for men who had not been vaccinated within the last six years to be re-vaccinated. (Auth: A.D.M.S., 9/9/15).	
9-12 a.m. 11th "		
9.30 a.m. 12th "	Church Parade.	
9-12 a.m. 13th "	Routine Training; Field Operations. Capt.Alston appointed President of standing Medical Board of the Brigade vice Lieut.Col.Warrack. (Auth; A.D.M.S., 10/9/15). Morning Sick to be seen at 7 a.m. N.C.O's. of Corpl's. rank and upwards granted permanent passes till midnight.	
2-4.30 p.m. "		
9-12 a.m. 14th "	Routine Training; R.A.M.C. Training, Physical Drill; Route March. Guard to be mounted at 2 p.m. and remain on duty for 24 hours; Day Police Picquet discontinued.	
2-4.30 p.m. "		

Army Form C. 2118.

WAR DIARY
or
INTELLIGENCE SUMMARY.

(Erase heading not required.)

Instructions regarding War Diaries and Intelligence Summaries are contained in F. S. Regs., Part II and the Staff Manual respectively. Title pages will be prepared in manuscript.

Hour, Date, Place	Summary of Events and Information	Remarks and references to Appendices
Sept.		
9-12 a.m. } 15th Balmer	Routine Training; Field Operations.	
2-4.30 p.m. } Camp,		
9-12 a.m. } 16th Falmer,	Routine Training; Physical Drill, R.A.M.C. Training, Route March.	
2-4.30 p.m. } SUSSEX.	Transport Inspection.	
9-12 a.m. 17th "	Routine Training; Squad Drill, Route March.	
2-4.30 p.m.		
9-12 a.m. 18th "	Routine Training; Company Drill, R.A.M.C. Training. Kit Inspection.	
9.30 a.m. 19th "	Church parade.	
9-12 a.m. 20th "	Routine Training; R.A.M.C. Training. Route March for "A" and "C"	
2-4.30 p.m.	Sections. B Section Bearer Sub-Division parade for Night Operations.	
8.0 p.m.	B Section Tent Sub-Division prepare an Operating Tent for reception	
	of "Wounded". Night Operations carried out successfully.	
9-12 a.m. 21st "	Routine Training; Improvised Carriage of Patients, Physical Drill.	
2-4.30 p.m.	C.O's. parade.	
9-12 a.m. 22nd "	Routine Training; Route March, R.A.M.C. Training.	
9-12 a.m. 23rd "	Routine Training; Company Drill, R.A.M.C. and Physical Training.	
2-4.30 p.m	Medical Inspection by Section Officers. Transport Inspection by O.C.	
	Permanent passes to all below the rank of Sergeant cancelled.	
9-12 a.m. 24th "	Routine Training; Route March in Morning.	
2-4.30 p.m.		
9-12 a.m. 25th "	Routine Training; R.A.M.C. Training, Physical Drill. Kit Inspection.	
9.30 a.m. 26th "	Church Parade. Percentage of men allowed on leave at once ordered 10%.	
9-12 a.m. 27th "	Routine Training; R.A.M.C. Training, Physical Drill. "A" and "B" Section	
2-4.30 p.m.	Route March. Night Operations for "C" Section as for "B" Section on	
8.0 p.m.	the 20th.	
9-12 a.m. 28th "	Routine Training; R.A.M.C. Training, Physical Drill. C.O's. parade.	
2-4.30 p.m.		
9-12 a.m. 29th "	Routine Training; Route March, R.A.M.C. Training.	
2-4.30 p.m.		
9-12 a.m. 30th "	Routine Training; R.A.M.C. and Physical Training; Improvised Methods	
2-4.30 p.m.	of Carrying Patients.	

Captain, Officer Commanding
2/2nd H.C.F.AMB. R.A.M.C.(T).

Army Form C. 2118.

WAR DIARY
~~INTELLIGENCE SUMMARY~~
(Erase heading not required.)

Instructions regarding War Diaries and Intelligence Summaries are contained in F.S. Regs., Part II and the Staff Manual respectively. Title pages will be prepared in manuscript.

Hour, Date, Place			Summary of Events and Information	Remarks and references to Appendices
	1915.			
9-4 p.m.	Oct.1st,	Balmer	Brigade Route March.	
9-12 a.m.	2nd	Camp,	Routine Training and Kit Inspection.	
9.0 a.m.	3rd	Falmer,	Church Parade.	
9-4.30 p.m.	4th	Sussex.	Routine Training during the day for B and C Sections. A Section Bearer and Tent Sub-Divisions parade at 8 p.m. for Night Operations.	
9-4.30 p.m.	5th	"	Routine Training and practice loading wagons with equipment. Cold Shoers return from course of instruction. Period of "Special Vigilance," ordered by Brigade. Men on Special Leave recalled and all other orders governing such periods carried out.	
9.0 a.m.	6th	"	Brigade Route March to Rottingdean. Field Ambulance inspected by Major General Young. Return to Falmer.	
9-4.30 p.m.	7th	"	Routine Training. Pte. Bailey discharged medically unfit.	
9-4.30 p.m.	8th	"	Routine Training.	
9-12 a.m.	9th	"	Routine Training and Kit Inspection.	
9.0 a.m.	10th	"	Church Parade.	
9-4.30 p.m.	11th	"	Routine Training.	
10.0 a.m.	12th	"	Inspection of the Field Ambulance and Camp by Surgeon General Culling.	
9-4 p.m.	13th	"	Routine Training.	
9-4.30 p.m.	14th	"	Routine Training. Transport Inspection.	
9.0 a.m.	15th	"	Brigade Route March. 26 Mules taken on charge by the Unit.	
9.0 a.m.	16th	"	Routine Training and Kit Inspection.	
9.0 a.m.	17th	"	Church Parade. Transport Inspection at 11 a.m. Posted in Daily Orders from Gazette, 16/10/15: "Home Counties Field Ambulance:— Captain W.E.Alston, M.D., to be Temporary Major (September 12th)."	
9.0 a.m.	18th	"	Routine Training.	
9.0 a.m.	19th	"	Routine Training. Section Officers supervise packing of wagons ready for change of station. Men instructed to pack up. Advance and Rear Parties detailed.	
9.0 a.m.	20th	"	Packing of wagons continued.	

WAR DIARY
or
INTELLIGENCE SUMMARY.
(Erase heading not required.)

Army Form C. 2118.

Hour, Date, Place		Summary of Events and Information	Remarks and references to Appendices
1915.			
8.0 a.m. Oct.21st	Balmer Camp, Falmer, Sussex.	Cook's wagon packed. 8.15 a.m., Transport moved off. 8.45 a.m., Field Ambulance moved off in marching order with Brigade for change of Station. Halt for night at Uckfield.	
8.15 a.m. 22nd	"	Route March to Sevenoaks. Halt for night at Tunbridge Wells.	
8.15 a.m. 23rd	"	Arrival at Sevenoaks. Motor Transport Driver A.S.C. taken on strength. B Section Nursing Orderlies detailed for duty at St.John's V.A.D. Hospital. C Section Nursing Orderlies remain on duty at Field Ambulance Headquarters at Kirkella. Wagons unpacked.	
9.0 a.m. 24th	"		
9.0 a.m. 25th	"	Routine Training, Fatigue duties, etc. A Section Nursing Orderlies detailed to attend at Cornwall Hall V.A.D. Hospital for duty.	
9.0 a.m. 26th	"	Routine Training, etc.	
9.0 a.m. 27th	"	Routine Training, etc.	
9.0 a.m. 28th	"	Routine Training, etc.	
9.0 a.m. 29th	"	Routine Training, etc. Bathing parade.	
9.0 a.m. 30th	"	Routine Training, etc.	
9.0 a.m. 31st	"	Church Parades.	

W. Welsh

Major,
Officer Commanding
2/2nd H.C.F.AMB. R.A.M.C.(T).

Army Form C. 2118.

WAR DIARY
INTELLIGENCE SUMMARY.
(Erase heading not required.)

Instructions regarding War Diaries and Intelligence Summaries are contained in F.S. Regs., Part II. and the Staff Manual respectively. Title pages will be prepared in manuscript.

Hour, Date, Place	Summary of Events and Information	Remarks and references to Appendices
November, 1915. Kirkella, Sevenoaks, Kent.		
3rd. Sevenoaks.	During the month the Unit has been engaged chiefly upon Nursing Duties, Guard Duties and Fatigues, Field work having practically ceased since the Unit left Balmer Camp, Falmer. The paucity of Medical Officers continues. The arrangement by which the Nursing Orderlies of two Sections are detailed for duty at the St. John's and Cornwall Hall V.A.D. Hospitals is still in vogue and additional Nursing Orderlies have been appointed for duty at the Headquarters Hospital, Kirkella. A Standing Medical Board meets every Wednesday, presided over by the Officer Commanding the Field Ambulance, who also discharges the duties of Senior Medical Officer to the 201st Infantry Brigade and to other Units in the Sevenoaks area.	
8th. "	The three Section Cooks detailed to attend a Course of Cookery instruction at Central Force School of Cookery.	
8th. "	Order posted that all entries relating to Inoculation and Dental Work to be put on last page of A.F. B.178 (Medical History Sheet).	
" "	In accordance with Divisional Order 650, 6/11/15, the Field Ambulance based their establishment on War Establishments Part IX., T.F., 2nd line. Tent and Bearer Sub-Divisions and Transport Sections adjusted accordingly.	
16th "	The first batch of men needing glasses visits optician at Tunbridge Wells.	
21st "	In consequence of the threatened prevalence of Scabies and Pediculosis, Officers Commanding Units were ordered to arrange for weekly inspection by Medical Officer in charge of Units.	
" "	W.O. Letter No.19/General No./5488 (A.G.2.B.) 2nd Nov.,1915, posted in Daily Orders with a view to urging time-expired N.C.O's. and Men to remain with colours until the end of the war.	
22nd "	Two men discharged and re-enlisted unto R.F.C. under the authority of W.O. telegram 5267, A.G.2.B. 3/11/15.	
23rd "	Second party of men requiring glasses visits optician.	
25th "	Inspection by Dental Inspecting Officer.	
27th "	Visit by A.D.M.S., 2nd Army, who expressed satisfaction after inspection of Hospital.	
" "	Brigadier General E.H.Molesworth,C.B., assumes Command of the 201st Inf.Bde. vice Lieut.Col.J.C.Worthington.	

O.C.,
2ND H.Q. 2ND FIELD AMBULANCE,
R.A.M.C. (T.)

Army Form C. 2118.

WAR DIARY
or
INTELLIGENCE SUMMARY.
(Erase heading not required.)

Instructions regarding War Diaries and Intelligence Summaries are contained in F. S. Regs., Part II. and the Staff Manual respectively. Title pages will be prepared in manuscript.

Hour, Date, Place	Summary of Events and Information	Remarks and references to Appendices
December 7th. Kirkella, Sevenoaks.	Transport Inspection by Assistant Inspector of Remounts, on Transport Field, Oak Lane. The Inspecting Officer expressed satisfaction with the condition of the horses of the Field Ambulance. W.A.	
" 8th. "	Travelling Medical Board visited Kirkella, and classified men of the Brigade. W.A.	
" 15th. "	Dental Inspection by the Dental Inspecting Officer. W.A.	

W. Allen

Major,
Officer Commanding
2/2nd H.C.F.Amb. R.A.M.C.(T).

Army Form C. 2118.

WAR DIARY
or
INTELLIGENCE SUMMARY.
(Erase heading not required.)

Instructions regarding War Diaries and Intelligence Summaries are contained in F.S. Regs., Part II. and the Staff Manual respectively. Title pages will be prepared in manuscript.

702/16
2 FEB 1916

Hour, Date, Place	Summary of Events and Information	Remarks and references to Appendices
January 12th, "Kirkella," Sevenoaks.	Inspection by Surgeon General Gulling. Afterwards the Surgeon General wished it to be notified to all ranks that he was very pleased with all that he saw both at "Kirkella" and at the inspection of the men and transport. W.W.	
" 18th, "	Visit by the Dental Inspecting Officer. One hundred men examined. W.W.	
" 28th, "	Inspection of horses of the Field Ambulance Transport by the A.D.V.S. who expressed his satisfaction with the condition of the animals. W.W.	

W. Walken
Major,
Officer Commanding
2/2nd H.C.F.A. R.A.M.C. (T).

Army Form C. 2118.

WAR DIARY
or
INTELLIGENCE SUMMARY.
(Erase heading not required.)

Instructions regarding War Diaries and Intelligence Summaries are contained in F.S. Regs., Part II. and the Staff Manual respectively. Title pages will be prepared in manuscript.

Hour, Date, Place	Summary of Events and Information	Remarks and references to Appendices
February 10th, 1916. "Kirkella," Sevenoaks.	Visit by the Inspecting Dental Officer.	
February 10th, 1916. "Kirkella," Sevenoaks.	Captain H. C. Barr gazetted to the 2/2nd H.C.F.Amb. and posted to "C" section.	Corps Order 187/16.
February 22nd, 1916. "Kirkella," Sevenoaks.	Move by train to Ipswich.	Corps Order 235/16.

Major,
Officer Commanding,
2/2nd H.C.F.Amb.;
R.A.M.C.(T).

www.ingramcontent.com/pod-product-compliance
Lightning Source LLC
Chambersburg PA
CBHW081515160426
43193CB00014B/2694